ALLEN PHOTOGRAPHIC GUIDES

D0351592

ALL ABOUT RUGS

CONTENTS

WHEN TO RUG

THE HORSE'S COAT

The majority of a horse's body is covered with hairs which are constantly being shed and replaced by newer ones. These hairs form the horse's coat, which is completely changed twice a year when he moults. In order to rid himself of these unwanted hairs the horse will roll, especially during moulting. Hairs grow from follicles within the outer layer of the skin, which also contain sweat and sebaceous glands, nerves, tiny muscles and

pigment. The sebaceous glands are tiny sacs connected to the hair follicles. These sacs produce an oil which helps keep the coat waterproof and the hairs pliable.

When a horse is exposed to cold, wet and windy weather he will soon develop a thick 'winter coat'. This coat is made up of an outer layer of coarse guard hairs, with an insulating layer of soft hairs underneath. Together with a layer of oil secreted from the sebaceous glands, these hairs provide a practically impenetrable coat that offers protection against the worst of winter weather. This being the case, you might be wondering why we bother to rug horses at all!

The reason horses often need to be rugged, is because we frequently remove the effectiveness of their coats, or even remove their coats altogether. We do this by:

- grooming them to such an extent that we remove their 'weather shield' by removing the protective oils from their coat;
- bathing them;
- stabling them so that they are not exposed to cold weather at the times when normally their coat growth would be triggered;
- breeding 'finer' horses, that have simply not evolved to endure harsh weather conditions;
- clipping them.

THE HORSE OUTDOORS

The time of year, how you keep your horse and what you do with him, will dictate whether or not he needs to be rugged. If your horse is a hardy sort (one of native or at least part native breeding) and is provided with a shelter and adequate food, the chances are he will not require a rug. However, by rugging your horse you can save both time and money. Your horse will stay cleaner, consequently being ready for work when you need him, and because he will be warmer he will require less food to maintain his ideal bodyweight.

THE STABLED HORSE

Stabled horses are rugged for two main reasons: to keep them warm and to keep them clean. Obviously horses do not require rugs to keep them warm through the summer months, but they may be rugged all year round in order to keep them clean.

THE CLIPPED HORSE

It follows that if you have removed a horse's natural coat by clipping him, you will have to replace it in some way. While there are other methods, such as using heat lamps, the safest, most convenient and cost effective way is by rugging. A clipped horse will need to be rugged both in the stable and field and sometimes when exercised.

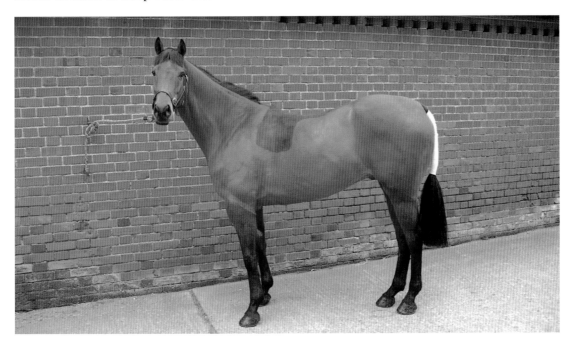

WHICH RUG?

Buying a new rug can be an expensive business, so it is necessary to choose carefully. However, rugs come in a bewildering number of styles, fabrics and colours, so selecting the most appropriate one, or ones, might prove a little difficult unless you know exactly what it is your horse really needs. The main points to remember when selecting a rug are that the length, depth and shape are correct for your *individual* horse, so that it will keep him warm and dry in all the right places. Then it is just a case of making sure you fit it correctly and look after it properly. A quality rug is usually a good investment, provided it is well cared for in line with the manufacturer's instructions.

TYPES OF RUG

In past years a horse required a whole wardrobe of rugs: one for the night when in the stable, one for the day, one when turned out in the field, another when travelling and so on. Now, with the development of modern fabrics, the whole business of rugging horses has become much simpler resulting in the need for fewer rugs. However, with rugs, as with most horse equipment, the old adage 'you only get what you pay for' is very true. Many rugs appear to be similar but their prices can differ enormously. This is usually due to the variance in outer fabrics used. For instance, many rugs have a 4 oz nylon 'outer', while the superior but more expensive rugs usually have a polypropylene, Cordura or ballistic nylon outer, which all offer a higher degree of tear resistance and durability.

A rug's 'inner', or lining, also needs consideration. *Breathable* nylons are better than cotton which has a tendency to promote rot and mildew as it holds moisture. If you are looking for warmth, you can choose a fleecy breathable liner, whereas a cooler option would be a breathable nylon net lining. Due to the advancement of fabrics it is possible to choose the type of rug with the sort of outer and lining that suits your horse's rugging requirements best, so do not be told that 'all rugs do the same job'.

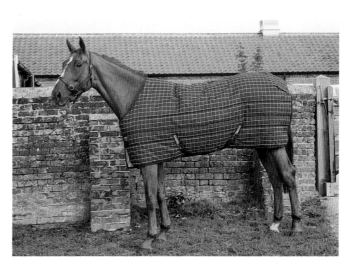

STABLE RUGS

Stabled horses are forced to stand idle for much of the time so warmth is a very important consideration when choosing a suitable stable rug. Comfort is equally important as the horse will be wearing his stable rug for most of the day and night. Virtually all modern stable rugs are made of a padded or quilted material with a nylon, polypropylene or Cordura outer and a cotton, or modern breathable lining, while traditional stable rugs were made of jute with a woollen liner. Many modern rugs are very lightweight but, due to the use of specifically designed fibres which have unique reflective thermal properties, they are still able to keep the horse warm even in temperatures below freezing. Stable rugs come in degrees of warmth, varying from heavy quilts for winter use, down to light-weight quilts used for travelling and to keep a horse clean in summer.

  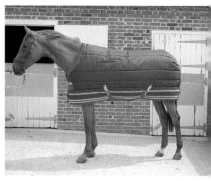

UNDERBLANKETS

When the weather turns extremely cold, stable rugs can have further layers added underneath for extra warmth if needed. Traditionally, ordinary blankets were used but these need to be put on very securely otherwise they will slip back as the horse moves or lies down (see page 20).

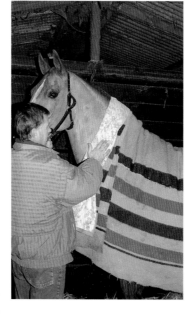

Alternatives for under-blankets include another, more lightweight, stable rug, a summer sheet, or a special-ly made clip-in underblanket which is designed to complement certain types of rug. These purpose-made underblankets are excellent, provided they are fitted correctly (see page 21).

NEW ZEALAND RUGS

New Zealand rugs are designed to keep a horse warm and dry while he's turned out in the field. Most New Zealand rugs are made of waxed cotton or canvas that needs to be re-proofed once or twice within a season to ensure no seepage occurs. The depth of New Zealand rugs is all important, for protection as well as preventing them from slipping. The sides of the rug should be long enough so that none of the horse's belly is visible. This will ensure that the rug is self-righting after rolling, and will protect the horse in all weathers. Traditional New Zealand rugs have hind leg straps, and some also have front leg straps as well. With a New Zealand rug, you need to fit the hind leg straps so that they are not too tight (in which case they will rub when the horse moves) or too loose (when the horse can get his hooves through them when he lies down). Link one strap through the other, and adjust them both until the width of your hand fits between them and the horse's legs. Having done them up ask someone to walk your horse on and view the straps from the rear – do they allow free movement?

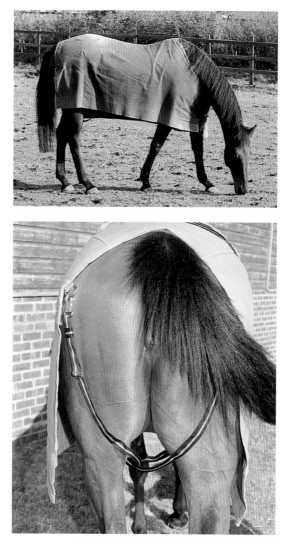

TURNOUT RUGS

Turnout is a term that *can* mean a rug is suitable for permanent wear, *or* that it is only intended for a stabled horse who is turned out for short periods. However, the latter is correctly known as a paddock rug, so check specific usage before you buy. Turnout rugs are mostly made of synthetic materials and, as with New Zealand rugs, their purpose is to keep the horse warm and dry while out in the field. Modern turnout rugs tend not to have any leg straps but are shaped over the quarters and come with a

tough fillet string and cross surcingles to keep them in place. As long as the rug is deep enough, this design works extremely well and is especially good for horses who object to rear leg straps or have sores due to previously poorly adjusted ones. Modern turnout rugs also have the advantage over canvas or waxed materials in that they are lightweight, come in degrees of warmth and tend not to rub the horse's shoulders. Turnout rugs designed for permanent use are completely waterproof, but at the same time allow moisture or perspiration to be

transmitted to the outside of the rug. Therefore the horse can still maintain and regulate his body temperature as he would through his natural coat.

You will eventually get seepage with any outdoor rug, but designs that have a seam running along the horse's backbone, will yield quite quickly. Those with seams three-quarters of the way down each side are far better, as a degree of seepage here will cause very few problems. While traditional canvas materials need to be proofed in order to made them water resistant, modern fabrics work on a hydrophilic proofing system. This is where the horse's own body heat activates a molecular action that wicks moisture away from the horse's body, while the rug's outer shell remains water resistant.

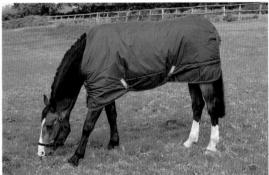

RUG TERMS

Some other terms which you will find in literature about outdoor rugs are:

Ripstop this indicates that the rug is made of a tough man-made fabric which will prevent many of the small tears made by branches etc. However, it is not a guarantee that the rug will not rip – barbed wire will rip anything!

Extra deep this usually refers to traditional New Zealand rugs and simply means that the rug is longer on each side of the horse than an ordinary rug.

Self righting such a rug will fall back in to place after rolling or excessive movement. It has leg straps, rather than cross surcingles, which are responsible for pulling the rug back into place.

Breathable this type of rug has a water resistant membrane under the outer fabric of the rug which permits vapour to pass through the fabric and then evaporate.

DAY RUGS

In days gone by the horse would have had his jute night rug changed for a lighter day rug. This practice has largely been dispensed with as modern fabrics are both lightweight and breathable, so the one rug does for night and day.

TRAVELLING RUGS

Traditionally, travelling rugs were made of wool and while you can still buy these, most people now use either a cooler in warm weather, or a light- or medium-weight stable rug for colder weather.

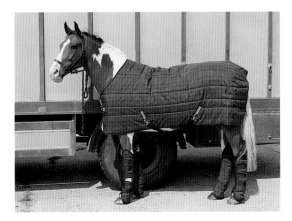

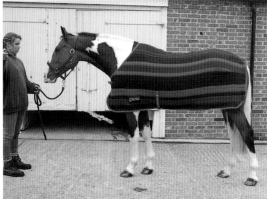

SWEAT RUGS

These look like large string vests and are designed to cool the horse off and prevent him from getting a chill after work, or when wet. The important thing to bear in mind when drying a horse off in this way, is that a sweat rug alone is not sufficient. They are designed to cool the horse by encouraging the evaporation of moisture but, unless the weather is particularly hot, the horse is also likely to get a chill. To prevent this, you need to form an insulating layer of warm air by placing another lightweight sheet over the top. The front can be folded back to encourage air flow, and the whole secured with a roller. However, always

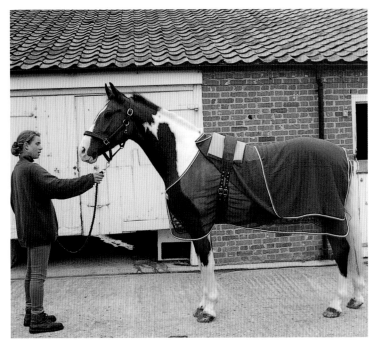

ensure that where a roller is used, it has padding underneath and that the rug is not wrinkled up at the girth.

COOLERS

Coolers fulfil a similar role to sweat rugs but with only one rug. Most modern coolers are specially designed to take moisture away from the horse and are therefore ideal for winter use as they can be put on the horse while he is still damp. They also double as summer stable/travelling rugs, so are a good money saver too!

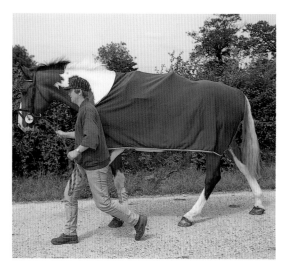

SUMMER SHEETS

These are usually made of cotton, but can be made of polypropylene or Cordura to match stable rugs, and are either used in the field during the summer to keep the sun and flies off the skin of a sensitive horse, when travelling, or just as a measure to keep dust off a stabled horse.

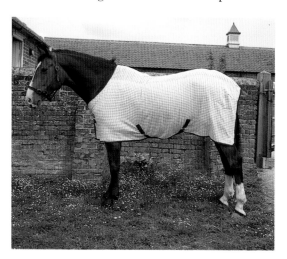

EXERCISE SHEETS

To prevent a clipped horse from getting cold while being exercised during the winter months, an exercise sheet can be used. This will prevent the horse's muscles from becoming cold and thus prone to cramp. They may be made of wool or of waterproof fabric or even fluorescent material which is ideal when riding on the roads in dull winter conditions. They are put on forward of the withers, the saddle is put on over the top and the front corners of the sheet are tucked well up under the girth straps. This allows for air circulation, but also keeps the horse's loins warm. Make sure the sheet is pulled well up into the gullet of the saddle, to prevent it from putting pressure on the spine during exercise. Some designs have a hole cut in them to accommodate the saddle, which then allows the saddle to rest on the horse's back as normal.

RUG ACCESSORIES

ROLLERS

Dramatic improvements in rug design over the past decade have almost eliminated the need for rollers. The one exception is where an anti-cast roller may be used to prevent a horse from rolling over in his stable (see page 14). However, where a rug does not have its own sewn-on surcingles, or where independent underblankets are used, a roller will be needed to secure it.

Rollers have a padded wither section, which is often put on over a foam pad to prevent localised pressure points. They run right around the horse and should be accommodated comfortably in the sternum curve (where the girth does up). They need to be done up firmly in order to prevent the rugs from slipping, but not as tightly as a girth. Generally, you should be able to place the flat of your hand between the roller and the horse's sides.

SURCINGLES

These do the same job as a roller, but are not padded at the wither and are often not as wide. It is essential to use a wither pad with surcingles to prevent excessive pressure. They are only suitable for temporary use, such as when securing a sweat rug. Surcingles placed over saddles during cross-country events for added security are known as cross-country surcingles.

CROSSOVER SURCINGLES

These are sewn onto the rugs, so you simply need to bring the rear strap on the offside to the front fixing point on the nearside, and the front strap on the offside to the rear fixing point on the nearside. On a correctly fitting rug these will cross over in the middle of the horse's belly. Crossover surcingles are now widely accepted as the safest and most secure way of fastening a rug to a horse.

FILLET STRINGS

These are used to prevent the rug from flying up over the back of the horse in windy conditions. They should be fitted fairly loosely under the tail but hang no lower than the end of the dock.

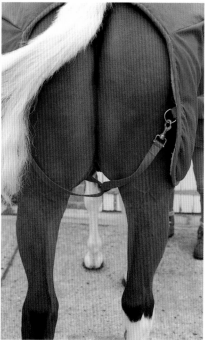

LEG STRAPS

These are usually only found on outdoor rugs, sometimes at both front and rear, but more usually only at the rear. They should be linked through each other and fixed back onto the clip on their own side to provide extra stability and to prevent them from getting caught on the hocks. To prevent chafing you can slip fleece sleeves over them, or gel sleeves which are waterproof but still soft. It is essential to keep these straps clean and supple.

ANTI-CAST ROLLER

As its name suggests this helps to prevent the horse from becoming cast. It is a fairly hefty piece of equipment comprising a leather roller with padded wither sections to which a leather covered, metal loop is attached. The idea being that the horse cannot roll over while wearing one and cannot therefore get stuck against the wall. In the main they are very successful at achieving their aim, but care does need to be taken with their use. In all cases a dense wither pad needs to be placed under them.

HOODS AND NECK COVERS

These are used as a means of controlling heat loss, or for preventing a horse from getting muddy while out in the field, although opinions vary as to the ethics of this – it is, after all, one of the horse's greatest pleasures! Some are simply hoods or neck covers which cover only the head or neck respectively, while others have neck cover and hood combined. Many rugs have matching neck covers and hoods and if you need to use one then it is best to select these as they should have all the necessary fastenings. However, if heat loss is your main concern there is a new design called a Wug, which is a turnout rug that goes half way up the horse's neck enclosing the shoulder, thus preventing rain from entering the front of the rug. This collar or scarf-like effect prevents the heat escaping

from the neck and shoulders making it a very warm rug in the worst of weathers.

If your rug does not have a matching hood then you can buy one separately. Some are loose fitting, simply draping over the neck and being secured by tapes or straps on the underside, while others are made of a light, stretchy material which is pulled on like a rubber glove. Some horses object to wearing these stretchy type of hoods, so go carefully if you attempt to fit one to your horse.

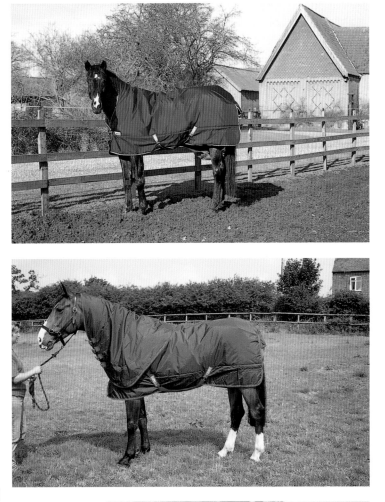

ANTI-RUBBING VESTS

These are used under rugs to prevent them from rubbing bald patches at the shoulder which is very common on horses living out full time wearing traditional New Zealand rugs. They are usually made of a stretch Lycra fabric which is pulled on over the neck, with a roller sewn on to secure it just behind the withers.

FLY VEILS

There are various types of veil and fly fringe. Most are used to prevent flies from irritating sensitive horses while out at grass. However, you will also see some horses wearing ones that completely cover the ears while competing indoors, in order to prevent them from becoming overwhelmed by the noise.

CORRECT FITTING AND USE

RUG SIZING

Irrespective of type, a correct fit is all important if the rug is to stay in place and be comfortable. Rugs are usually sized in 3 in increments starting at around 3 ft 6 in up to about 7 ft. This measurement refers to the length from the centre of the chest around the body to the rear of the quarters where the rug ends. However, there are no hard and fast rules as to what size of rug will fit what height of horse as a broad horse may need a bigger rug than a thinner one of the same height, or perhaps a differ- ent make or style which might be a more generous fit. To ensure you get the right size of rug, take the four measurements on your horse as shown and then measure the rug in the shop before purchasing. You may find the rug's length is exactly right but the depth is incorrect; or the neck depth is right but the length is wrong and so on. Keep measuring rugs until you find one that is exactly right. You may find that your horse will require one size larger for his turnout rug than for his stable rug.

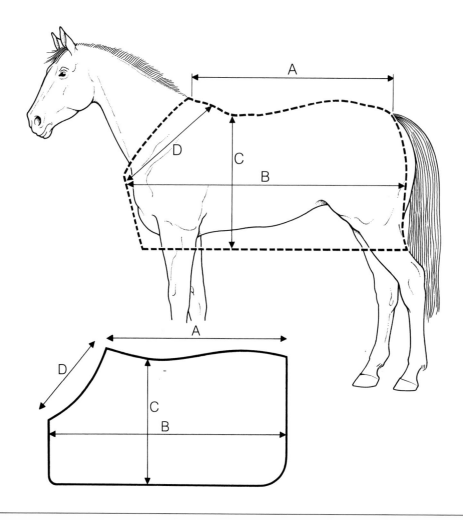

RUG FITTING

Having got the right size it is important that you put it on and fasten it correctly. While the older horse might tolerate you throwing a rug straight over its back, a younger or more nervous one will not appreciate it at all, so it is sensible to always practise a **safe rugging technique**.

1. Before putting on a rug, fold it in half by bringing the back up and over the front, so that the inside lining is facing outwards. Gently lay this over the neck and wither area.

2. Carefully fold the rug backwards over the quarters.

3. Once it is in place check that both sides are level so that one side does not hang lower than the other.

4. Do up the chest straps, but do not pull the rug forward in order to do so as this will pull the hair the wrong way and make the horse uncomfortable. If you find the rug is too far back, then take it off and replace it further up the neck, repeating steps 1 – 3.

5. A lot of rugs have insufficient overlap at the chest. The front fastenings should allow the rug to close neatly together across the chest, without being taut. A secure type of rug may have a Velcro strip at the chest which allows for a snug fit, with added security being provided by slip buckle fastenings which do up over the top. This allows for individual fitting, ensuring an optimum fit for each and every horse. If your

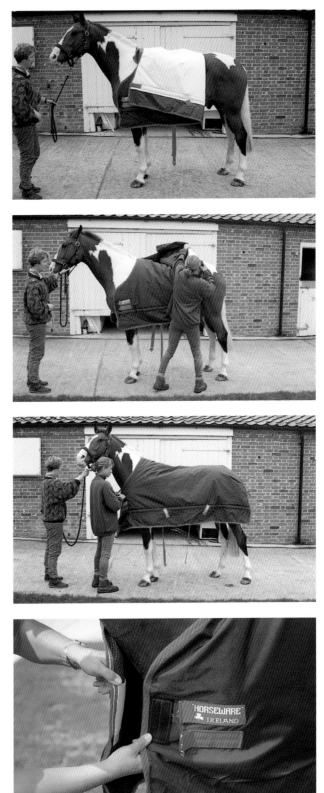

horse has a very deep chest, chest extenders are available from certain manufacturers.

6. Getting the tension right for the roller or crossover surcingles is very important. They should be done up firmly enough to prevent the rug from shifting, but not as tightly as you would do up a girth. As a guide, you should easily be able to slip a fist between the straps and the horse's skin.

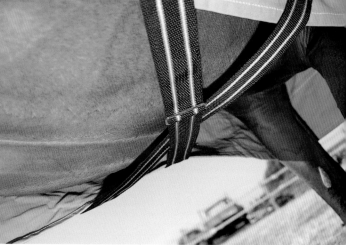

7. Once everything is done up, the rug should look 'right' – stand back and take an overall view.

POINTS TO CHECK FOR A GOOD FIT

- **The withers** A well fitting rug should lie about 2 – 4 in in front of the withers.

- **The shoulders** To allow for free movement from the point of the shoulder, the outside edge of the rug should be well in front of the shoulder. The front should not be too tight as it has to allow for the horse putting his head down to the floor. As a guide, the top strap should be in line with the point of the shoulder. When the horse is standing still with his head tied up you should be able to get the width of two hands between your horse's chest and the straps.

- **The rump** The rug should finish just as the tail starts (unless the rug incorporates a tail flap). If the rug flops over the tail then it will have a tendency to slip, whereas if the rug falls short of the tail the horse will become cold. The rug should also be a snug fit over the rump. This is achieved by darting, so that it fits the contours of a horse's quarters.

- **The belly** You should not be able to see it!

RUG TIP

When trying on a new purchase, fit it over the top of a summer sheet so that if it does not fit properly you can return it in a clean state.

FITTING TRADITIONAL UNDERBLANKETS

The tendency to use ordinary bed blankets is now diminishing in favour of purpose-made underblankets for horses. However, if you find you have to fit ordinary blankets, it is essential they are put on in a safe way.

1. Fold the blanket in half and with the open end towards the horse's head lay it over his neck. Fold it back until it comes to just in front of the base of the tail. The blanket should still be three quarters of the way up the horse's neck.

2. Fold each front corner up to the withers to form a point on the neck.

3. Put on the stable rug and secure as normal.

4. Fold the point back along the withers securing it with a roller and pad. Make sure that the point is flat and not crumpled up as this will put pressure on the withers and make the horse's back sore.

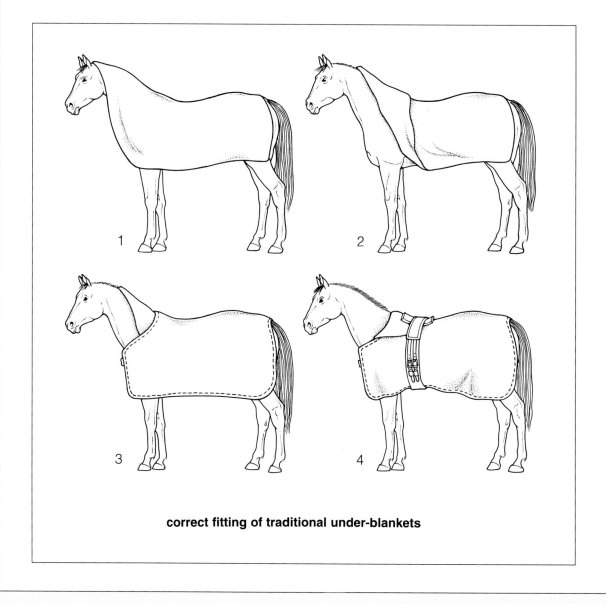

correct fitting of traditional under-blankets

PURPOSE-MADE UNDERBLANKETS

When using a purpose-made underblanket, make sure it is secured to the stable rug in line with the manufacturer's recommendations. If these are not available, you should fasten both rugs together with the fillet string as shown.

SPECIAL FEATURES

Many rugs incorporate special features such as anti-open buckles, buckle covers and tail flaps. In the main these are added benefits, but the first consideration *must* be a correct fit. Which rug you choose thereafter will depend upon personal preference.

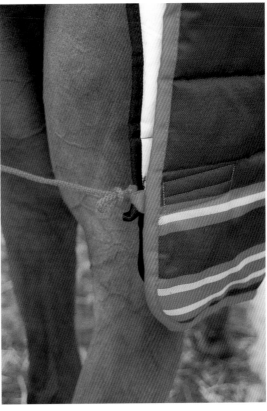

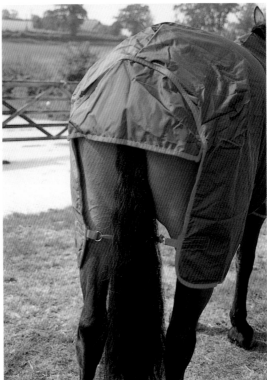

PROBLEM SOLVING

RUBBING AND SORES

The areas most prone to rubbing and sores are the shoulders, withers and hips. Damage may be caused by:

- the rug putting pressure on one or more of these parts;
- the rug slipping and therefore chafing vulnerable parts;
- the rug moving back and forth as the horse moves.

In all cases the cause is an ill-fitting rug. The ideal solution is to change the rug for one that fits perfectly. If this is not possible, you can line the shoulders, withers, or hip points with sheepskin, which will help to make the horse more comfortable, but will not alter the real cause. If you do use sheepskin (or a similar fleecy lining) do

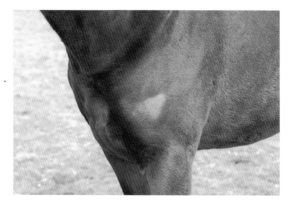

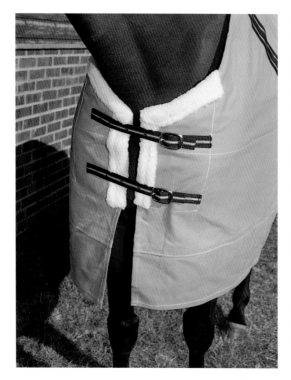

make sure it is brushed regularly and kept clean. Some horses have the sort of shoulder conformation that appears to make them vulnerable to rubbing whatever type of rug is used. In this case, an anti-rubbing vest (see page 15), will definitely help.

If the rug requires a roller to fasten it, and it is this which is rubbing the horse's withers, you really should invest in a rug with crossover surcingles.

SLIPPING

This may be caused by the horse's conformation but, again, most likely it is because the rug is not an ideal fit. Rugs that require a roller are more likely to slip than those with crossover surcingles. Make sure that you have fitted the rug properly and that the roller or surcingles are neither too tight, nor too loose (see pages 12–13). Similarly, if the rug has leg straps ensure these are correctly adjusted.

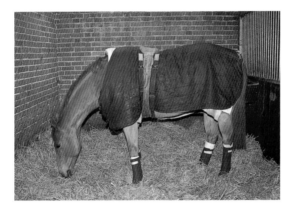

RUG TEARING

Rug tearing, or at best a horse that undresses himself, is a fairly common vice, usually caused by boredom. A good preventative measure is to fit the horse with a 'bib'. These are made of hard plastic or leather and attach to the horse's headcollar under the chin. It prevents him from being able to grab hold of the material in his

teeth. If the horse still manages to tear the rug while wearing one of these, a bar muzzle may be the only solution, although this is not ideal as it does make eating more difficult.

Alternatively, the horse can be roughed off over the winter months so that rugging is not necessary, although obviously this may not be an option if the horse is finely bred, or must be kept in work.

RUG SHYNESS

Some horses can behave quite badly when being rugged. However, the fault usually lies in the horse's past experiences of rugging. Either the first person to rug him up was inconsiderate enough to simply throw the rug over his back and thus scare him badly, or the horse's rug may have been fitted so badly that it caused him constant discomfort.

The solution is to first ensure the horse's rug is a perfect fit and second to practise a safe rugging technique at all times. Follow the steps on pages 17–19, and take it very slowly at first, introducing the rug over a period of days, rather than minutes. It may take you a little time to rebuild your horse's confidence, but once you have shown him there is nothing to hurt or scare him he will no longer be in fear of being rugged.

ACKNOWLEDGEMENT

Thank you to Horseware Ireland for supplying the rugs for the equine models.

British Library Cataloguing-in-Publication Data.
A catalogue record for this book is available from the
British Library

ISBN 0.85131.675.1

Published in Great Britain in 1997 by
J. A. Allen & Company Limited,
1 Lower Grosvenor Place, Buckingham Palace Road,
London, SW1W OEL

Design and Typesetting by Paul Saunders
Series editor Jane Lake
Printed in Hong Kong by Dah Hua Printing Press Co. Ltd.